YUKON MEMORIES

BY

KAREN J SIMON

Yukon Memories

By Karen J Simon

First Edition ©2016
Revised 2020

No part of this book may be copied, scanned, downloaded, transmitted, printed or reproduced in any form without express written permission from the author.

Front cover photo by Karen J Simon
Back cover Photo by Karen J Simon
Photos by Howard Hess and Karen J Simon

Published by Create Space

ISBN numbers:
ISBN-13:978-1535557962
ISBN -10:1535557966

Dedication

This book is dedicated to my son Rodney and to my granddaughter Ariel. The only two of my family I ever traveled through the Yukon with. I traveled the Alaska Highway with Rodney twice – In 2002, he accompanied me on tour Fairbanks to Skagway and Feb 2003 we drove Fairbanks to Seattle. It had been years since I had spent any quality time with my son and on these two trips I came to know the young man I had raised. I am proud of you, my son. Ariel asked me to travel with her and her husband when they moved from Alaska following his military tour. It was her first such long trip by car. We made some wonderful memories along the road. I love you Ariel.

Acknowledgments

I have been writing since I was a child. At first I hid my writings because I was afraid of the reaction of others. When I was in the fifth grade my mother found one of my stories and shared it with a teacher who asked me where I learned to write. I read a lot , I study the book as I read and when I wrote my own stories, I tried to emulate what I read. Around that same time, I read a book about Stradivari that left a profound impression of imprinting pictures in the mind with words and I wanted to do the same thing. Thank you Mom and Mrs. Wetterling for the first approval of my writing.

I am not a professional photographer and I am not a great artist but I try to combine knowledge of the two when I take photos. I try to impart a sense of feeling; combining both to enhance each other. I know that I have succeeded when others encourage me to do more. Without that support and encouragement, none of my books would exist. The list of names would seem endless so all I can say is a heart felt thank you to all.

Mystic Alaska – my first self published book was intended only to share the year round beauty and daily life of Alaska, but those who saw it wanted a copy. They made it a success.

I Believe - was first published in the mid 90's at a local Fairbanks print shop – a 5 x 7 book with no photos or paintings but it was a huge success. A few years ago, my friend and publisher, Robert Jacobson, encouraged me to rewrite the original version and add paintings. It took almost 5 years to complete the project but it, too, has received good reviews.

When I share a success story with my son, his remark is always, "Right on, Mom. Way to go!" There is no better encouragement than that.

One book leads to another as ideas are discussed and friends, family and coworkers encourage the project. My travels as a tour bus driver have taken me to many places in Alaska and the Yukon. There is so much history, the beauty of nature is so overwhelming and the land is overflowing with geological events that beg to be investigated and shared. In this book I have only touched the surface of any of this. Thanks to all of those at home and at work who have encouraged me to keep on writing.

Encouragement from my granddaughters is deeply appreciated. Thank you Jordan, Ariel and Jenna.

TABLE OF CONTENTS

The Yukon………………………………………………………………1

Spell of the Yukon………………………………………………………2

Yukon Memories……………………………………..………… …4

Poker Creek – Top of The World…………………………….... …..8

George Black Ferry ……………………………………………..…9

Klondike Gold Rush…………………………………………….......11

Gold Dredge #4…………………………………………………….12

Dawson City, Yukon Territory……………………………………13

Moose Hide Slide…..……………………………………………….15

Klondike Mines Rail Road…………………………………….......16

S.S. Keno…..……………………………………………………….17

Tintina Trench……………………………………………….........18

Yukon Silver………………………………………………………..19

Watson Lake……………………………………………….............20

Beringia……………………………………………………………..21

Whitehorse………………………………………………………...22

Robert Service……………………………………………………..23

S.S. Klondike……………………………………………………....24

Klondike Cargo…………………………………………………….25

On Board the S.S. Klondike ………………………………….......26

Wind Indictor……………………………………….…………….27

Yukon River…………………………………………… ……..……28

South Klondike Highway………………………………………...29

Carcross, Desert…………………………………………………...30

Carcross, Yukon Territory…………………………………………31

Chilkoot Pass & Lake Bennett…………………………………….33

S.S. Tutshi………………………………………………………….34

White Pass Yukon Railroad……………………………………….35

Montana Mountain…..……………………………………………37

Canyon Creek Bridge..38

Haines Junction..39

Yukon Flowers...40

A Glimpse of Yukon Wildlife.....................................42

Sheep Mountain...42

Kluane Lake...44

Destruction Bay...45

Highway Monument..45

Burwash Landing...47

Mount Churchill..48

Alaska Highway...49

Beaver Creek...50

Yukon Winter..51

Bibliography..54

THE SPELL OF THE YUKON

I wanted the gold, and I sought it;
 I scrabbled and mucked like a slave.
Was it famine or scurvy—I fought it;
 I hurled my youth into a grave.
I wanted the gold, and I got it—
 Came out with a fortune last fall,—
Yet somehow life's not what I thought it,
 And somehow the gold isn't all.

No! There's the land. (Have you seen it?)
 It's the cussedest land that I know,
From the big, dizzy mountains that screen it
 To the deep, deathlike valleys below.
Some say God was tired when He made it;
 Some say it's a fine land to shun;
Maybe; but there's some as would trade it
 For no land on earth—and I'm one.

You come to get rich (damned good reason);
 You feel like an exile at first;
You hate it like hell for a season,
 And then you are worse than the worst.
It grips you like some kinds of sinning;
 It twists you from foe to a friend;
It seems it's been since the beginning;
 It seems it will be to the end.

I've stood in some mighty-mouthed hollow
 That's plumb-full of hush to the brim;
I've watched the big, husky sun wallow
 In crimson and gold, and grow dim,
Till the moon set the pearly peaks gleaming,
 And the stars tumbled out, neck and crop;
And I've thought that I surely was dreaming,
 With the peace o' the world piled on top.

The summer—no sweeter was ever;
 The sunshiny woods all athrill;
The grayling aleap in the river,
 The bighorn asleep on the hill.
The strong life that never knows harness;
 The wilds where the caribou call;
The freshness, the freedom, the farness—
 O God! how I'm stuck on it all.

The winter! the brightness that blinds you,
The white land locked tight as a drum,
The cold fear that follows and finds you,
The silence that bludgeons you dumb.
The snows that are older than history,
The woods where the weird shadows slant;
The stillness, the moonlight, the mystery,
I've bade 'em good-by—but I can't.

There's a land where the mountains are nameless,
And the rivers all run God knows where;
There are lives that are erring and aimless,
And deaths that just hang by a hair;
There are hardships that nobody reckons;
There are valleys unpeopled and still;
There's a land—oh, it beckons and beckons,
And I want to go back—and I will.

They're making my money diminish;
I'm sick of the taste of champagne.
Thank God! when I'm skinned to a finish
I'll pike to the Yukon again.
I'll fight—and you bet it's no sham-fight;
It's hell!—but I've been there before;
And it's better than this by a damsite—
So me for the Yukon once more.

There's gold, and it's haunting and haunting;
It's luring me on as of old;
Yet it isn't the gold that I'm wanting
So much as just finding the gold.
It's the great, big, broad land 'way up yonder,
It's the forests where silence has lease;
It's the beauty that thrills me with wonder,
It's the stillness that fills me with peace.

THE YUKON

The Yukon - as mysterious and alluring as Alaska – is one of the youngest parts of Canada, but - like Alaska – it is the oldest continuously inhabited part of North America. Both are part of a geographical area now known as Beringia that extended from the Lena River in Siberia to the McKenzie River in Northern Canada. Genetic evidence supports the theory that people lived isolated in Beringia for thousands of years before migrating eastward to the area now known as Alaska and the Yukon. Archeological sites near the village of Old Crow in northern Yukon show that they may have arrived here as early as 10,000 BC.

Like Alaska, the Yukon was largely ice free during the last ice age and, like Alaska, has, because of its northern location, both continuous and discontinuous permafrost. That permafrost has played a role in shaping the development of industry and population growth in the Yukon.

The triangular shaped Yukon covers 186,661 sq. miles which is slightly larger than the state of California (156,299 sq. mi.). British explorer John Franklin was the first European to visit the Yukon in 1825. Fur traders Robert Campbell and John Bell arrived in 1840, claimed the land for the Hudson Bay Company and built several trading posts on the Yukon River. Around 1846, they began calling the land 'Yukon'; a name which appears to be derived from the Gwich'in word 'Yu-kun-ah' meaning 'great river'. Depletion of fur bearing animals caused world markets to look at other materials and as demand for silk increased, demand for fur decreased. British colonies in Canada signed a confederation in 1867 creating the first provinces and the following year took over control of the Hudson Bay land claims. Gold miners began arriving in the territory and in order to stay in business, the Hudson Bay Company branched into new ventures. The Yukon Territory was first governed as part of the Northwest Territories but split away as a separate territory in 1898.

News of a gold discovery near the confluence of the Klondike and Yukon Rivers brought thousands from all over the world rushing to strike it rich. The first city of the gold rush – Dawson – became, in one month, the largest city north of Seattle and west of Winnipeg with a population of 40,000. It served as the territorial capitol from 1898 to 1952 when the population went below 5,000 and the capitol moved to Whitehorse. In 2012, the total Yukon population was 36,304.

World War II brought new life to the Yukon with military bases, road and oil line construction. These resulted in the discovery of more minerals which increased mining and called for more people, service needs and eventually tourists. Mining includes the production of zinc, lead, silver, gold, iron, uranium and copper. Farming has not been a huge factor due to climate, terrain, ground conditions, high cost and limited transportation but new technology is increasing the possibilities of increasing farm production.

Rich in natural resources, the Yukon also has one of North America's largest grizzly population (6,000 - 7,000) and Dall sheep (estimated 19,000) and approximately 22,000 mountain sheep. Other big game population includes black bear at about 10,000; moose population is estimated at about 70,000; caribou at 250,000 and wood bison around 1,500.

Official flower of the Yukon - fireweed.
Official bird - raven.
Official tree - sub-alpine fir.

YUKON MEMORIES

If there's a land that captures the imagination, the Yukon has to be at the top of the list. As a child, I remember Jack London's 'Call of the Wild' and an early television show called 'Sergeant Preston of the Yukon'. The Klondike Gold Rush gave us Johnny Horton's song 'North to Alaska' followed by a movie starring John Wayne that was based on the song. And somehow, Alaska and the Yukon became synonymous, leading a large number of people to believe that the Klondike is either part of Alaska or another name for Alaska.

The Klondike, the Yukon, the gold rush… land, history, dreams, legends, tragedy, success, failure and hope. Robert Service said it well – that there is a lure to the land…vast, beautiful, unpeopled, wild and untamed…imbued with a sense of peace.

I was excited the first time I headed for the Yukon…I was going to step on the land of legends whose snowcapped mountain peaks I had seen in the hazy distance from mountain top roads on tour to the remote village of Eagle on the banks of the Yukon River in Alaska.

The old customs house in Eagle stood on the high bank above the river and I loved visiting it from the very first. I had the impression, as I walked through the cool interior with late afternoon sun slanting through dusty windows, that I had stepped back in time. Old ledgers were open on the high counter, inkwells were capped and a pair of round metal rimmed glasses set aside awaiting the return of a diligent officer come morning. I pulled the old ledger closer and read some of the entries – the names of boats with their captain's name listed, passengers - if any, cargo, duty fees, port of origin and port of destination. One entry listed a canoe that brought in several copies of a banned book (I believe it was entitled - 'A Miner's Life') – that cargo was confiscated and the trial date and presiding judge was listed as was the court ruling on the case. On the wall just inside the front door was a page of information that I returned to take note of, and, over all the years I drove tours through Alaska and the Yukon, I quoted that information because I found it fascinating.

When I first started driving tours, the company I worked for owned a 50 passenger jet boat that took passengers from Eagle, Alaska to Dawson, Yukon Territory. It seemed like an interesting trip and I had hopes that one day I would be able to do it. But I couldn't afford a hotel in Dawson and I didn't know anyone there I could stay with and then there were the daily chores at the end of the tour – sweep and mop the interior of the coach, take care of the dump tank and wash the outside of the coach. Many of the other drivers went on the boat – I just could not bring myself to justify the costs, so I watched it come and go with a yearning deep inside.

The following summer, the boat crew began to invite me on the trip, but I continued to hold back. Then one day as I was helping them unload baggage from the coach, they told me that today I had no choice - I was going to Dawson. I started with my usual protest, "I can't, I have no place to stay in Dawson."

"Oh yes, you do!" they stated. "We have an extra room at the crew house."

"But, the bus…" I started.

They cut me off. "Pay one of the kids to clean the coach!. Where's your bag? When you bring the passengers back, we're holding the boat for you; the van will follow you back to town while you park and then you're coming with us!"

With a bit of trepidation, I talked to the local high school student who was our guide that day and he agreed to take care of the coach for me. I hastily grabbed everything I needed and jumped into the van.

That was not the last trip I took to Dawson but it changed the flavor of all my tours. Every person I met coming off the boat in Eagle was excited and enthused about what they had just experienced, but as I welcomed them to Alaska and the United States, I assured them that they could never tell their relatives, neighbors and friends back home about the trip they had just completed. That statement was met by stunned silence and then I continued – "I've done that trip and I don't believe that you can find the words to describe the scenery, the experience, the emotions that you have had today. All of your photos will diminish the size and scope of what you've seen; they will look like a postage stamp version of what you actually saw. You have to experience to understand it because words and photos can't begin to describe it. I believe that if Mark Twain had ever floated the Yukon River, we'd have our very own Yukon Huck and Tom."

Dawson was not what I expected, but I fell in love with it. Nestled on the banks of the Yukon River at the confluence of the Klondike River, it is dwarfed by the hills surrounding it. In 1997, there were no paved streets in Dawson and there are still no cement sidewalks. The streets were graveled which was still an improvement over the mud the early miners slogged through. The sidewalks are all boardwalk. I call Dawson, 'the town that time forgot'. A good number of buildings date back to the gold rush; some have been restored and some sadly show the passing of time, hoping for the same. Present building codes require new ones to conform to that era's architectural style in order to keep the frontier mining town a tourist calling card to the history of the past.

The past comes alive in Dawson. The bank where Robert Service worked stands unused and abandoned on a corner of the main street. The can can girls still spin their skirts and kick their legs high at Diamond Tooth Gertie's Dance Hall and Casino where all proceeds go toward restoration and upkeep of the old buildings. 'Robert Service' recites his best known ballads in the yard near his cabin and down the street Jack London's cabin looks as it did when he was in residence. Every year a writer earns the chance to spend the winter in Pierre Burton's cabin in hopes of finding inspiration for their own writing. All over town guides dressed in period garb relate the history of the early tent city and the people who made it into a city of renown. Dawson was once the capital of the Yukon and the government buildings are as well kept now as they were then.

I had dinner with one of the crew and got a brief tour around town, but they had early hours so we weren't out long. By the time I got up next morning they were all gone. They had left me breakfast rolls and coffee with a note reminding me of departure time. Before I left, I wrote a huge THANK YOU across the white board on the kitchen wall, collected my bags and walked down to the boat landing.

If the trip upriver in the evening light had been awesome, the downriver trip was beyond words. I had spent some time in the wheelhouse the day before and I went back up to start the trip down. Captain Al was eager to share the workings of all the instruments and equipment and, once out in the main channel, would allow one to take the wheel for a bit.

The Forty Mile River empties into the Yukon just east of the Alaska border and when we approached the confluence, Captain Al shut down the engines and we floated. Below decks, one of the crew started a recording – Robert Burns reciting Robert Service's 'The Spell of the Yukon'. Robert Burns was an Irishman who lived in Dawson and performed at the Service cabin where he literally became Robert Service. Robert's rich Irish brogue seemed to make Robert Service come alive as the bagpipes softly played Amazing Grace in the background. Above, the sky was clear and blue – without a cloud, a plane or vapor trail. As we drifted, the silent boreal forest on either side slipped by – no buildings, no traffic sounds, no barking dogs – no indication of civilization. Then the voice stopped and the strains of bagpipe music faded away and there was only silence except for the sound of the silt laden water beneath the boat and along the high stone walls on one side. The passengers stood rapt as if in church; there wasn't an eye on board that didn't show the sparkle of a tear. The moment passed, the engines came to life and the boat swung back into the main current but the passengers remained hushed and humbled.

The Yukon River is the fourth longest river in the world, third longest in North America; the longest in the Yukon and Alaska. Its headwaters flow from beneath the glaciers of snow covered peaks in the mountains just about 17 miles north of Skagway, Alaska. It flows northwest through the Yukon Territory and Alaska to empty its waters into the Bering Sea, 2,220 miles away draining an area of about 328,000 square miles.

Now let's get back to the information on the wall of the old customs house that I found so fascinating. They keep track of water flow in the Yukon River. During open flow season (May through Oct.), 1.1 million gallons of water per second flows by Eagle, Alaska. That 1.1 million gallons of water is carrying 2.4 tons of silt per second. Said like that it doesn't seem quite so impressive, but lets look at it from a different angle. 2.4 tons of silt per second times 60 for a minute, times 60 for an hour, times 24 for a day, times 7 for a week, times 4.3 for a month, times 5 for open flow season. Keep in mind that a lower volume of water flows beneath the winter ice so flow is really 12 months. It has been over 100 years since the miners came down that river…so… is there a mountain missing? And if so…is there more gold to be found? But more interesting than that is that the Yukon River is moving Canada to the western coast of Alaska at the rate of 2.4 tons per second. For a couple of years I ran tours to Prudhoe Bay on the Haul Road north of Fairbanks and we routinely stopped for lunch at the Yukon River Crossing. On one such tour, while the passengers were eating lunch I took the coach down to the river to wash mud off the windows. There was a crew from the University of Alaska Geophysical Institute taking water flow measurements and I asked for figures. Half way across Alaska, inflowing streams and rivers had increased water flow to 1.5 million gallons per second and silt to 2.9 tons per second.

It would be another year before I made it to Whitehorse and the city captured my heart the first visit. Lying on a strip of land between the bank of the mighty Yukon and the white bluffs above, it seems to have held some of the gold rush aura that drew the prospectors north. A modern city, it is unique in that it does not have a dead city core. The center of town is as active and alive as it was in the days of the gold rush; Main street is still main street. Old buildings have either been refurbished or replaced with new ones that blend in with them. The railroad no longer comes to Whitehorse, but the station which served the miners now serves mushers as headquarters for the Yukon Quest 1,000 mile International Dogsled Race and tourists who ride the trolley across the old waterfront. The SS Klondike no longer sits at dock waiting for eager miners going north to the gold fields; instead, she sits in dry dock at river's edge waiting for the throngs of visitors eager to learn about the gold rush and walk her decks trying to imagine the atmosphere and bustle of those early riders facing an uncertain future with none of the comforts of todays life but whose life and hope hinged on striking it rich in the Klondike gold fields.

In the years that I have traveled the Yukon – both winter and summer – I have come to love the land as if it were my own. I have traveled the North Klondike from Dawson to Whitehorse and the South Klondike from Whitehorse to Skagway during summer months and the Alaska Highway from Delta, Alaska to Dawson Creek in Canada during winter months. Robert Service captured the land in his words in the Spell of the Yukon. As a tour driver, these are the memories of the north that I encourage my passengers to take home.

Ah! There's the land. (Have you seen it?)
It's the cussedest land that I know…
From the big, dizzy mountains that screen it…
To the deep… deathlike valleys below.
Some say God was tired when He made it;
Some say it's a fine land to shun;
Maybe… but there's some as would trade it
For no land on earth—and I'm one.

There's a land where the mountains are nameless,
Where the rivers all run - God knows where;
There are lives that are erring and aimless…
And deaths…that just hang by a hair;
There are hardships that nobody reckons;
There are valleys - unpeopled and still;
There's a land—oh, it beckons and beckons…
And I want to go back—and I will.

There's gold - and it's haunting - and haunting…
It's luring me on as of old;
Yet - its not having the gold that I'm wanting…
So much as - just finding the gold…
It's that great – big - broad land - 'way up yonder…
It's the forests - where silence has lease;
It's the beauty - that thrills me with wonder…
It's the stillness - that fills me with peace.

Poker Creek – Top of the World Highway

GEORGE BLACK FERRY

My first trip to Dawson by road was another adventure. The Taylor Highway into Eagle washed out due to flooding so motor coaches were sent over the Top of the World Highway with passengers who had originally been scheduled to travel by jet boat. The Canadian Customs officer noted that my coach did not have the proper plate nor did I have the proper paperwork, but knowing the circumstances that brought us this route, he said, "We'll just call this an emergency evacuation of Eagle!"

From its junction with the Taylor Highway at Jack Wade Junction, the 79 mile long Top of the World Highway winds across the crest of a mountain range which is part of the Yukon Tanana Uplift. Then, from an elevation of over four thousand feet it descends to the Yukon River across from Dawson City. There is no bridge over the Yukon River on the Top of the World Highway - the river is crossed by ferry, a ride which takes six to seven minutes. When I came home from that trip, I showed a photo of the ferry to my son (a semi truck driver); he told me that there was no way I put a 45 foot bus on that little ferry. I had to admit that it was a daunting feat. I had never put a coach on a ferry and I had heard that the ferry was small, but was not prepared for exactly how small - I was more than a bit nervous and more so when the ferry swung into the current and I am sitting at the wheel knowing I have no control!

Right – Ground crew prepares for George Black ferry landing on Top of the World Highway across the river from Dawson.

Above- George Black Ferry loading at the end of the Top of The World Highway across from Dawson City, Y.T.

Right - View from the driver seat on board the ferry – the ferry has yet to swing around into the current and turn to begin the up river crossing to Dawson.

Prior to 1901, a small steamer took passengers back and forth across the Yukon River at Dawson. During the summer of 1900, with a profit of $200.00 a day (($5,000.00 in 2019 dollars), the steamer could not keep up with the demand.

The 1897 gold rush brought John Hubrick to the Yukon – broke. He mined claim 34 Above Discovery and by 1901 was said to be worth about $100,000.00 In 1901, John bought supplies and built a cable ferry on the Dawson waterfront; the cable tower, completed in 1902 became the tallest man-made structure in the Yukon. The cable was anchored 16 feet below Third Avenue, then rose to the top of the 36 foot tower that straddled Front Street just south of Queen Street before spanning the Yukon where it was anchored to the rock bluff on the opposite shore. Hubrick tried unsuccessfully to sell the ferry to the government for $14,000.00 during the two years it was in operation even though he never made any money. A major fire in 1904 damaged the cable anchoring and repairs were estimated at about $4,000.00. Hubrick offered it to the government for $8,000.00, but again hey refused so he sold it to D. A. Matheson for less than eight. Matheson turned around and sold it to the government for $13,400 which raise immediate questions about corruption. Despite all of that, repairs were made, and the ferry went back into operation. A spring flood in 1944 damaged the cable tower and the system was dismantled and a power boat pushed the ferry back and forth across the river. In 1946, the landing was moved to its present location.

When the Cassiar Asbestos Corp. opened the Clinton Creek asbestos mine near the confluence of the Yukon and Fortymile rivers in 1966, they offered to pay half the cost of a bridge across the Yukon River at Dawson City. In 1966 the bridge would have cost three million dollars; by 2006, the cost had climbed to about 39 million. Rather than invest in a bridge, the government chose to purchase a $25,000 ferry boat with an operating cost that would eventually reach one million dollars per year.

Built in Vancouver, B.C. by Allied Shipbuilders in 1966, the ferry was cut into ten sections for shipment to the Yukon. From Skagway, the sections were loaded onto the White Pass & Yukon Railroad for transport to Whitehorse. Five weeks later, the ferry was reassembled and launched on June 8, 1967 for the downriver run to Dawson. Twice, the ferry grounded on sandbars, the first as it approached Lake Laberge just north of Whitehorse and the second, nine miles out of Dawson. Crews of the Public Works Dept winched it off the first sandbar, the ferry McQuesten pulled it off the second. It arrived in Dawson City on June 14th.

The Top of the World Highway is closed during winter months, but an ice road allows access from Dawson City to West Dawson. Except for a two hour shut down for maintenance in the early hours of Wednesday, the ferry operates 24 hours a day from early May to late October or early November – depending on ice flow in the river. As ice thickens, the ferry is slid out of the water on wooden ways to the top of the dike until next season.

Approaching Dawson City landing

Unloading at Dawson City landing

KLONDIKE GOLD RUSH

Robert Henderson prospected Rabbit Creek in 1896 and apparently found little of interest, so went over the hill to continue his search. Around the same time, George Carmack, Skookum Jim and Tagish Charlie were also prospecting in the area. On August 6, George found nuggets wedged in the crevices of long flat slabs of bedrock on the bottom of the stream. He filled a bag and headed for the boom town of Forty Mile some 60 miles down river. At Forty Mile – so the story goes – George went to the bar and proclaimed his discovery, but no one believed him until he reached into his shirt pocket, withdrew a bag and emptied its contents onto the bar. By morning Forty Mile was a ghost town, everyone had packed up and headed to Rabbit Creek. Miners descended onto the creek, staking claims and renaming it Bonanza Creek. Robert Henderson was one of the last to hear the news.

In June 1897, miners laden with gold from the creeks traveled to St. Michael on the western coast of Alaska and boarded the steamer ships Excelsior and Portland. The Excelsior docked in San Francisco on July 17th with half a million dollars in gold. Three days later, the Portland docked in Seattle carrying over a ton of gold worth a million dollars. News traveled around the world and started the largest rush for gold in the history of mankind. People from all over the world rushed to Seattle to begin the journey north to the Klondike gold fields. Unfortunately, by that time, most of the land had been claimed and a steady stream of gold was pouring out of the new boom town of Dawson City at the confluence of the Klondike and Yukon Rivers. In the mad rush for gold, men and women struggled up mountain passes, over land, sea and rivers leaving behind stories of heartbreak, tragedy, loss, success and wealth beyond the wildest dreams. It is estimated that 100,000 people made the attempt but only about 30,000 of them arrived in the Klondike and of those, only 4,000 actually found gold and only a few of them found a fortune. Some of the hardy survivors followed every rumor of gold hoping to find the illusive pot of gold at the end of the rainbow. Some of those followed the trail to Nome for the next big gold strike in 1898. A large number went home, broken and discouraged and a few remained to start businesses and build a new life in a new land.

Population in 1898 was 40,000 – by 1899, when the rush ended it was 8,000. The city incorporated in 1902 with a population under 5,000. It served as the territorial capital from 1898 to 1953. By 2013, the town of 1,375 retains its unique frontier appearance with no cement sidewalks and no paved streets.

Gold Dredge #4 on Bonanza creek near Dawson, Yukon Territory

Gold Dredge #4

Control Room – levers controlled bucket speed, digging angle, trammel speed, conveyor belt, dredge movement

Above – Overlooking washing trammel

Above – Dredge buckets lined up near dredge

Below – Looking up stacker where conveyor belt sent material out to tailing piles

Above – cables extending to control room and levers
Below – massive gears

Dawson City, Yukon

Dawson City – from the Top of the World Highway

Dawson City – from the top of the Dome

Dawson City – from the George Black Ferry

Above – Canadian Bank of Commerce

Above –Post Office

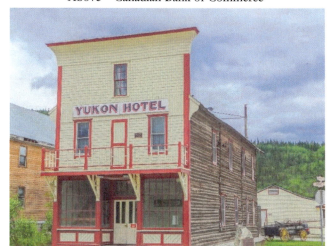

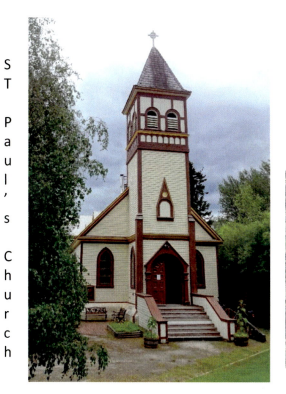

St Paul's Church

Robert Service Cabin

Jack London's cabin

Commissioner's home while Dawson was the capitol city

MOOSEHIDE SLIDE

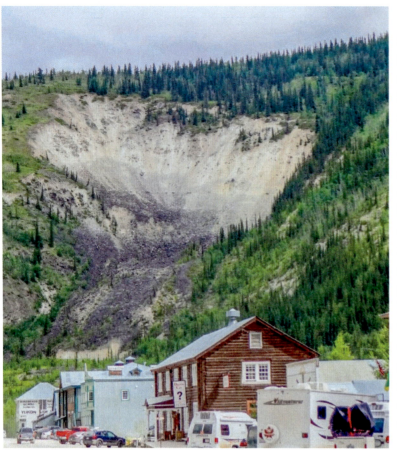

One of the most prominent land features in Dawson is the barren slope above the north end of the city created by an ancient land slide estimated to be about 2,000 years old. Such events tend to give rise to legends that attempt to explain the existence of the anomaly. The origin of this, like the event which created the strange formation, is buried in the mists of time. It is known as 'Moosehide Slide' because its shape looks something like an old stretched moosehide. According to one legend, raiders chased a local village man up the hill where he hid under trees near a pile of rocks and roots that had been prepared for just such an event. As the enemy warriors came closer, he pulled out the roots that had been used to stabilize the mass of rocks and roots releasing an avalanche that killed all but one of the raiders. The lone survivor took news of the event back to his own village.

Science, however, explains it differently. Dawson is located on a geological formation known as the Tanana Yukon Uplift. The Pacific Plate pushes against the North American Plate buckling it, and lifting it, as it drops down and slides under it. The Denali fault which arcs through the center of Alaska, lies between these two plates. Running north, at the eastern edge of this fault, is one of the greatest fault lines in western North America – the Tintina Trench. According to geologists, most major rivers follow fault lines and when you hear the geological history of Alaska, the Yukon and the Yukon River, you hear a lot of information about fault zones and formations caused by earthquakes.

Some of the rocks identified in the Dawson area are extremely old, belonging to some of the very early geological eras. Pressure, water and time have combined to create unstable formations in the earth in some areas and the hill above Dawson is one such place. The same forces that originally created the slide, are still at work and portions of the slide show evidence of slow but steady movement. At the top of the slide where the initial ground broke away and began to slump downward, tension breaks run parallel to the face exposing roots and splitting trees vertically. In the middle to lower section, sheared trenches, stretched roots and split trees are evidence of continual movement. Measurements from 2006 to 2011 show that the upper portion moved 1½ to 4½ feet per year while during the same period the lower portion moved 3¼ to 7 ¾ feet per year.*

* Brideau, M.-A., Stead, D., Roots, C., and Lipovsky, 2012. Ongoing displacement monitoring at the Dawson City landslide (Dawson map area NTS 116B/3). In: Yukon Exploration and Geology 2011, K.E. MacFarlane and P.J. Sack (eds.), Yukon Geological Survey, p. 17-26.

KLONDIKE MINES R.R.

In 1903, construction of the narrow gauge Klondike Mines Railway started in hopes of providing better transportation. Completed in 1906, it stretched nearly 32 miles from Dawson City to Sulfur Springs. The railroad operated four steam locomotives and two passenger cars as well as box cars and flat cars with a crew of four engineers, three firemen and six brakemen often providing 24 hour service to the mines. By 1913, reduction of mining, dredge shutdowns, fewer passengers and right of way payments created financial shortages that forced the closure of the railroad. The engines pictured here are in the Railroad Museum in Dawson.

Engine Number 1, one of the oldest locomotives in Canada, was built in 1881 by Brooks Locomotive Works in Dunkirk, New York for the Kansas Central Railway. In 1890, it was sold to Alberta Railway and then, in 1900, to the White Pass Yukon RR where it operated for 2 years. It was sold to the Klondike Mines RR in 1902 but sat idle until 1905. Intended only for construction, after completion of the mine railroad in 1906, it saw little use until it went back to Skagway to be used by WP&YR as a yard goat. In 1961, the locomotive was donated to the Dawson City Museum.

Engine #2 rolled out of the factory at Baldwin Locomotive Works in Philadelphia, Pennsylvania in 1885. Originally owned by Columbia & Puget Sound RR, it was sold to the White Pass Yukon RR in 1898. Klondike Mines RR acquired the engine in 1905. It was the primary engine for the mine until it ceased operations.

Right: Built by Baldwin Locomotive Works in 1899 for the White Pass Yukon RR, Engine #3 is the only remaining compound engine in Canada. Sold to Klondike Mines RR in 1906, this coal burning locomotive worked very little until 1910. Before it could begin operation, rock alongside the track had to be cut back because this - the largest and most powerful locomotive operated by the mine - was two feet wider than the others.

S. S. KENO

Sternwheelers plied the rivers of the Yukon and Alaska moving miners from one place to another, taking out gold and bringing in supplies. It is estimated that somewhere between 240 to 280 sternwheelers once operated on these northern waterways. Most of them are long gone, some exist as piles of old lumber amid rusty metal in sternwheeler graveyards; their names and stories long forgotten; decaying skeletons of the gold rush. Only three northern sternwheelers survived when modern transportation ended the need to operate them – two in the Yukon and one in Alaska.

Silver, as well as gold, was discovered in the Yukon, but a solid vein of silver was discovered on a tributary of the Stewart River in 1914. The big Yukon sternwheelers could not operate in the shallow waters of the river, so in 1922, the S.S. Keno was built in Whitehorse specifically for use on the Stewart River. For almost 30 years, she moved supplies into the area and took silver ore out to be transferred to larger vessels. The last steamer to run on the Yukon, she made her last voyage from the salvage yard in Whitehorse to her new berth in Dawson in 1960 with 21 passengers, most of whom were news media. Now owned by Parks Canada, the SS Keno is open for tours, though parts of the boast are closed due to need for repairs.

TINTINA TRENCH

View from the Tintina overlook on the North Klondike Highway south of Dawson

According to the continental drift theory, millions of years ago, plates of land collided to create the land masses we know today. Beneath the ground, fault lines mark the edges of broken plates, and along these lines, geological forces continue to reshape the land. Along the western coast of North America, plate collisions thrust land upward creating the Rocky Mountains and the Cascades. As the pressure eased and the land settled, valleys formed between the mountain ranges creating two of the greatest faults in western North America. The Rocky Mountain Trench (between 2 – 10 miles wide) - extends northward about 900 miles from western Montana through Canada to the southern Yukon and the headwaters of the Yukon River. The Tintina Trench, thought to be an extension of this rift, extends approximately 600 miles into the Yukon Flats in Alaska. The two trenches are separated only by the Liard Plain.

The Tintina Trench is a side slip fault, which means that plates are sliding past each other rather than lifting over or under each other. The plate on the south side of the fault is moving northward. Rocks that lie under Dawson were once next to the Ross River about 279 miles to the south east.

Landslides within the trench north of Dawson cause the most significant land changes. Originally, rivers in this area drained south into the Gulf of Alaska, however ice build up during the first ice age forced the rivers to turn west and north to empty into the Bering Sea. The instability of the land seems determined to slowly turn the rivers south again.

YUKON SILVER

In 1919, silver was discovered in Keno creating a boom and bust economy that lasted nearly 70 years. Though more than 600 claims were filed in 1920, the location was so remote that access was always an issue. The big Yukon River stern wheelers could not ascend the shallow, fast running Stewart River and the smaller boats could only get to Mayo – 35 miles short of the mines. In 1922, a caterpillar tractor train went into operation reducing the shipping cost, then, 2 years later a concentration mill was built allowing for the extraction of lower grade ore. During 1930, the Keno mine produced 3.7 million fine ounces of silver; 14% of Canada's total silver production. In 1932, silver prices collapsed but the main concentration of silver ore had been depleted in the Keno mine and, by 1934, the mine was shut down. In 1935, a rich vein was discovered nearby, the price of silver recovered and a new mill was built at Elsa (est. 1929). By 1939, the price of silver had collapsed again and the mines were once more shut down. Off and on mining kept the community going until the last Keno Hill mine shut down in 1989. This remote living ghost town is home to one of the Yukon's most comprehensive mining museums, an interpretive center, a remnant of historic buildings, and a small, but interesting, population of miners, old-timers and artists.

Mayo (est. in 1903) became the service hub for the remote mining locations in the Keno area. Large sternwheelers came up the Yukon to load silver, zinc and lead ore for shipment to Whitehorse and to drop supplies going into the mines. Riverboat was the only way in until a year round road was completed in 1950.

Outdoor washroom

WATSON LAKE

Watson Lake, the Yukon's third largest community, is the gateway to the Yukon when entering from British Columbia on the Alaska Highway. Founded as Fish Lake by Frank Watson in 1898, it began as a fish camp, but World War II changed all of that. The airport, built in 1941, was a major refueling stop for aircraft flying the Northwest Staging Route from Malstrom Air Force Base, Great Falls, Montana to newly built Ladd Field in Fairbanks. In 1942, the small community boomed with the arrival of thousands of soldiers arriving to build the Alaska Highway.

The signpost forest was started in 1942 by a lonely soldier who missed home and put up a sign that included mileage. Carl K. Lindley (1919 – 2002) of Danville, IL was a member of U.S. Army Company D, 341st Engineer Battalion, who had arrived to work on the road. The signpost forest has continued to grow as visitors add signs from all over the world. As of August 2010, there were more than 76,000 signs.

40 miles south of Watson Lake is Contact Creek at the border of the Yukon and British Columbia.

BERINGIA

Located just off the Alaska Highway on the bluff above Whitehorse stand silent sentinels of life that once roamed this land 20,000 years ago when ice covered much of the northern hemisphere. With so much water trapped in ice, the oceans were low enough that North America and Asia were part of one land mass. At one time, it was thought that only a very narrow land bridge connected the two continents but ground core samples and under water studies revealed that the bridge was a grassland that was estimated to be approximately 1000 miles across at its widest point. A variety of animals and man traversed this ice free corridor from Asia to northern Canada.

Relatives of modern day elephants once roamed the open grasslands between massive sheets of ice. Tusks were often unearthed during early mining operation in the interior of Alaska and the Yukon and are still found in the Yukon, Alaska and Siberia.

(Modern buildings and equipment have been removed from the photo of the mammoth pictured below)

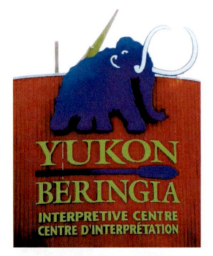

Wooly Mammoth

Ice age beavers were the largest known rodent in North America during the Pleistocene Age. The size of a modern bear, they could be anywhere from 6 to 8 feet in length, weighing up to 135 pounds. Though the Pleistocene beaver has general similarities to modern beaver, they are not close relatives. With its massive incisors it is easy to imagine the giant beaver as an ice age lumberjack felling trees in ancient forests, but science is unsure of its habits. Shape and chemical analysis of giant beaver teeth suggests that wood may not have been a part of their diet. It indicates that, much like our modern muskrat, they preferred herbaceous aquatic plants. It is most probable then, that they only lived in the Yukon during warm periods between ice advances when forests returned to the North.

Giant Beaver

WHITEHORSE

Whitehorse is one of my favorite cities. Nestled between the banks of the mighty Yukon River and the bluffs above, it is a mixture of frontier and modern. It is a rare city that held on to its heritage and grew without losing the health of its core. While residential and shopping areas spread beyond the original city lines, downtown Whitehorse remains the center of city life. Old buildings have either been torn down and replaced or restored and occupied. Government offices, Visitor Center, shops, banks, restaurants, tourist attractions and major hotels bring visitors and locals alike to historic downtown Whitehorse.

3 story log cabin in Whitehorse

After the dangerous passage through the Devil's Punch Bowl, Miles Canyon and Whitehorse rapids, weary gold seekers set up a ragged tent city on the east side of the Yukon River where they could regroup, rest and prepare for the journey north to Dawson and the gold fields.

In 1897, Copper was discovered on the western slopes western slopes of the Whitehorse Valley and the rag tag tent city began to move across the river. That same year, a 12 mile toll road was built up White Pass out of Skagway. Within a year, the road right of way was purchased by the newly formed White Pass & Yukon Railroad Company and rail construction started on May 28. The northern portion of the rail was completed in 1900 connecting the new settlement of Whitehorse on the west bank of the Yukon River with Carcross. Completion of the Carcross to Lake Bennet portion connected Whitehorse to the port of Skagway and ensured a secure future for the new city. It became the capital of the Yukon in 1953.

Sunset over Whitehorse

ROBERT SERVICE

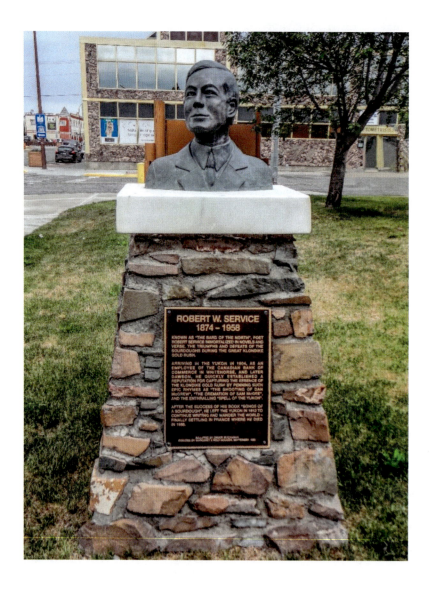

Robert W. Service, born in Preston, England went to work for the Commercial Bank of Scotland after leaving school. He had been writing since age six and sold verses while still in school. Fascinated by the life of a cowboy, he left England when he was 21 and lived in the U.S. and Mexico before going to Canada. Sometime after moving to Canada he went to work for the Canadian Bank of Commerce. They sent him to Whitehorse in 1904 and to Dawson in 1908. For the next 8 years he remained in the Yukon writing story poems about life in the northland in his spare time. He sent a collection of them to his father, who had moved to Toronto, asking him to have it published. 'Songs of a Sourdough' sold 1,700 copies before it was published. Sales of the book earned him more than $100,000. In today's money that would be about $2.5 million. It was the first of several very successful books.

Robert Service left the Yukon in 1912 and never returned. He passed away in France in 1958.

Known as the 'Bard of the North', Service is best known for 'The Cremation of Sam McGee', 'The Shooting of Dan McGrew' and 'The Spell of the Yukon'.

S.S. KLONDIKE

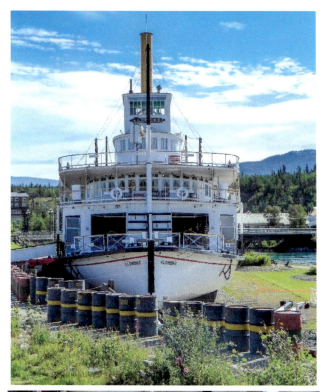

The *S.S. Klondike* was built in Whitehorse in 1929. Despite her shallow draft, she could carry 50% more cargo than any other boat on the river without the need to push a barge. June 12, 1936, the Klondike headed up river to Dawson. Turning around a point with a rock bluff on the left between Lake Laberge and Hootalinqua, she crashed into and slid along the bluff, tearing out the whole side. Another rock tore the steering lose. Afloat, but unable to steer, the Klondike drifted down river while the crew tried to get a line to shore, but the current was too strong. Whenever the boat drifted close enough to shore, a few passengers and crew jumped off. Nearly three miles down river, she finally came to rest on a sandbar. Salvage crews saved as much of the sternwheeler as they could and used it to build *Klondike 2* - identical *to Klondike 1*. The 1,300 ton, 210 foot long *Klondike 2* was launched in May 1937. Largest of the 250 boats that operated on the Yukon, she carried freight up and down the river until 1952 when the highway to Dawson was completed. She was converted for passenger tours, but by 1955, lack of interest and high operational costs left her stranded in the Whitehorse shipyard. Donated to Parks Canada in 1960, she was moved to her present location in 1966. Supported on greased rollers and with the aid of four bulldozers, a crew of 12 men and eight tons of Palmolive soap, the *S.S. Klondike* slid slowly over the streets of Whitehorse – a move which took three weeks to complete. On 24 June 1967, *Klondike II* was designated a National Historic Site. Renovation back to her 1937 state was completed in 1981 and she is now open for tours, looking much as she did when hauling freight.

KLONDIKE CARGO

On Board the S.S. Klondike

WIND INDICATOR

One of the largest weathervanes in the world is a DC-3. Serial #4665 was built in 1942 and then the US Army Air Force put it into service flying transport missions in India and China. At the end of the war, the DC-3 was sold to a new company - Canadian Pacific Airlines. Under new Canadian registration as CF-CPY, it was converted for civilian use. Almost ten years later it was sent to Whitehorse to serve in the Yukon. In 1960 it was sold and moved to Dawson where it serviced Old Crow as well as early seismic and oil exploration camps. In 1966, it returned to Whitehorse for scheduled and charter flights. Then, in November 1970, she lost an engine during a routine take off. Although take off was aborted without incident, CF-CPY was destined never to fly again. With a total of 31,581 flying hours, it was relegated to a hangar where it remained until October 1976, used only as a spare parts plane. When it was no longer useful for that, it was listed for destruction. An aircraft maintenance engineer proposed that the aircraft be placed at the entrance of the Whitehorse airport to serve as a monument to the history of Yukon aviation. By 1977, he had bought the old plane and sold it to the Yukon Flying Club for one dollar and the task of restoration. It was four years before CF-CPY was ready to face the elements again. A local businessman and welder suggested that the aircraft pivot on a pedestal and in 1981, it was successfully mounted alongside the Alaska Highway in front of the airport. It was removed for more restoration in 1988 and remounted in 2001. In 2009 the aircraft was taken from the pedestal again and both were moved to the present location in front of the Transportation Museum next to the airport. The aircraft is so precisely balanced that it requires a wind of only five knots (approx. six mph) to move.

YUKON RIVER

Fiver Finger Rapids in the Yukon River between Dawson and Whitehorse was one of the most dangerous portions of the river for sternwheelers. Five massive pillars of rock nearly blocked the river creating narrow channels through which water churned with such force that sternwheelers often had to wench through the only channel deep enough to navigate. From 1900 to 1927, rock was blasted enough to widen the river by 20 feet.

Miles Canyon near Whitehorse was a major obstacle during the gold rush. Water flowed into a wide section known as the Devil's Punch Bowl before entering the narrow channel between high stone walls. So many boats were lost here that the RCMP took control of all boat traffic through the canyon. No boat was allowed to proceed unless it had a number showing that it had been inspected, a qualified pilot was aboard and the names of all aboard recorded; no women and children were allowed.

Construction of Schwatka Dam on the Yukon River in 1958 raised the water level in the canyon reducing the turbulence of the water in the Devil's Punch Bowl. The higher water level, which also created Schwatka Lake, obliterated all traces of the Whitehorse Rapids for which the city was named. The world's longest wooden fish ladder was added in 1959 to help salmon migrate to spawning grounds at the headwaters of the Yukon.

SOUTH KLONDIKE HIGHWAY

The water of Emerald Lake just north of Carcross has a beautiful green hue created by light reflecting off deposits of white marl. Marl is a lime rich mud which contains variable amounts of clays and silt.

The headwaters of Lake Bennett are located in Northern British Columbia. The elongated lake stretches north into the Yukon, covering 23,919 acres (37 sq. mi.) with an average depth of 203 feet. The heart of the Southern Lakes system which makes up the headwaters of the Yukon River, it became one of the best-known because of the Klondike Gold Rush. Thousands of stampeders climbed the Chilkoot Pass in the Coastal Mountains from Dyea on the Lynn Canal to the shores of Lake Bennett. During the winter of 1897 - 98, the largest tent city in the world lay sprawled along the shore as tens of thousands stopped to build boats for the remainder of the journey north to the Klondike. After the arduous trek over the mountains, the gold seekers faced the high winds and rough waters for which Lake Bennett is famous. For 18 hours on May 29 and 30, 1898, more than 7,000 boats crossed the waters of the lake headed for the Yukon.

On the road to Carcross   Photo by Howard Hess

Rail Bridge across Nares Lake in Carcross

A rainbow hovers west of Lake Bennett at Carcross

Just outside of Carcross is the world's smallest desert (according to the Guinness Book of World Records) – the Carcross Desert. The one square mile, 640 acre bed of sand is not a true desert but the bottom of a large dried ancient glacial lake called Lake Watson which disappeared with the glaciers. Over time, the wind shifted the sand, creating dunes. The ecosystem of this unique desert, which is home to some rare plants and insects, is unstable and fragile - harsh winds and shifting sands destroy plants as the desert moves steadily northward. Delicate and fragile plants grow on the edge and crests of the dunes. Unusual plants, such as Baikal sedge and Yukon Pine, can be found among the dunes. Baikal sedge has been listed as a "threatened" species under the Federal Species at Risk Act. Only six remain in the Yukon, one in Alaska, and another in Asia. Yukon Lupine is a rare species of lupine that evolved in the dunes of both the Yukon and Alaska. Siberian asters are abundant in some of the most active portions of the dunes.

Ten or more species of insects in the Carcross Dunes are found in few other places on earth. Scientists have found eight species that may be new to science. The Coast Dart is a moth found in the dunes of Europe and Asia, Carcross and Alberta. The Dune Tachinid Fly is a rare insect which is restricted to a very small area of unglaciated Beringia in the southwestern Yukon and is a parasite of the larva of the Coast Dart Moth. Another moth - the Gnorimoschema is a small moth which lives in dry areas in the northern hemisphere. Five new species of these, found at Carcross in the 1980s, have not been scientifically described or named. Although winged and capable of flight, they run, hop and flutter across the sand. They are difficult to spot because their color blends with the sand.

CARCROSS, YUKON TERRITORY

Old beaches along the shore of Lake Bennett indicate that the site of Carcross was once submerged beneath about 400 feet of water. Flaked stone tools found in the area, estimated to be 4,500 years old, show the presence of First Nations People in this area long before the Klondike Gold Rush. Because large herds of caribou once migrated across Nares Lake twice a year, the area was originally called Caribou Crossing. In 1896, the arrival of the first gold seekers brought permanence to the small seasonal village. In 1902, Bishop Bompass had the name changed to Carcross because mail for the school he had established there was being sent to other places with the same name in the Yukon, Alaska and British Columbia. Skookum Jim, of the Klondike gold discovery, owned land in Carcross and negotiated one of the first land claim agreements in the Yukon when he agreed to allow the railroad to build across his land in exchange for jobs for people in the community. The 110 mile long White Pass Yukon Railroad, completed at Carcross in 1900, continued to call the station Caribou Crossing until 1916. Fire destroyed most of downtown on Christmas Eve 1909, but by 1910, buildings were moved from the deserted mining town of Conrad to replace those lost to the flames. Dawson Charlie Street, in Carcross, is now one of the last Yukon streets composed entirely of historic buildings that have remained relatively unchanged since 1910. The South Klondike Highway from Whitehorse to Carcross was begun in 1950 and completed to Skagway in 1978. Maintenance of the road to allow year round access is shared by Canada and the U.S. Today, tourists from around the world pass through Carcross following history and the trail of the Klondike Gold Rush.

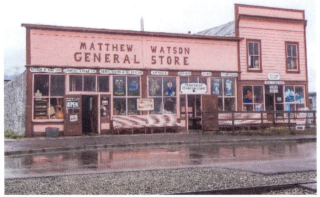

Carcross shops   Photos by Howard Hess

Above - Old Mountie office and jail

Photos by Howard Hess

The Yukon's most famous hotel – the Yukon Hotel - was built in Bennett in 1898. In 1901, it was loaded onto a scow and floated across the lake to Carcross where it was renamed the Anderson Hotel. Tagish Charlie, one of the first to discover gold in the Klondike, bought the hotel in 1903, renamed it the Caribou Hotel, made extensive renovations and operated it until his death in 1908. Ed and Bessie Gideon leased the hotel from his estate. It burned down in the Christmas Eve fire of 1909 and they rebuilt it the following year. Bessie died in 1933 and the hotel was rented out again until about 1940. It was purchased by May Ross who owned it until her death at 92. Bob Olson then owned and operated it until he was murdered in the hotel in 2004. New owners began renovation in 2007. It was dedicated as a Yukon Heritage Site in 2008. One of the oldest buildings in the Southern Lakes Region, it is one of the last two 3-storey frame Yukon commercial buildings dating from the early 20th century and was the Yukon's longest continuously operating food and lodging businesses.

Polly, one of the most famous hotel patrons, may have climbed Chilkoot Pass with the first stampeders. For a number of years, he lived at Conrad with Captain James Alexander, owner of the Engineer Mine. Captain Alexander and his wife planned a trip in 1918 and decided that Polly, who was about 50 years old, would stay at the Caribou Hotel. The Alexnders were aboard the Princess Sophia when it sank in the Lynn Canal. Polly stayed at the Caribou until his death. For 55 years, he sang opera in the hotel, spewed constant profanity and drank without paying, preferring scotch, cursing more if it was not served fast enough. He was widely and well known as the 'hardest-drinkin, best-swearin, dirtiest no good' in town. Near the end of his life, Polly gave up alcohol and cursed the odor of it. When he passed away in November 1972, at the estimated age of 126, a funeral train carried dignitaries and fans from Whitehorse to attend the

service. Following the service, Polly was laid to rest in the Carcross Pioneer Cemetery, but because he was a parrot, the government had to issue special permission to allow his interment there.

CHILKOOT PASS & LAKE BENNETT

Looking across Lake Bennet from Carcross

The Coast Mountains formed a formidable barrier to the Klondike gold fields from Skagway and Dyea on Lynn Canal. A Tlingit trading trail, the Chilkoot Trail was first used by gold prospectors in 1880. In 1883 Lieutenant Frederick Schwatka follwed the trail writing: *All around us was snow or the clear blue ice of the glacier fronts, while directly northward, and seemingly impassable, there loomed up for nearly four thousand feet the precipitous pass through the mountains, a blank mass of steep white...* He was talking about Chilkoot Pass – elevation 3,759 feet. From Dyea, the trail rose 900 feet to the base of the pass. Because packs were weighed and readjusted here, the area called the Scales. From this point, the ground, now consisting of sharp slabs of rock, rose steeply – five to six hundred feet in about half a mile and was so difficult during summer that crawling was often the only way to ascend. Here, during that winter, 1,500 narrow steps - the 'Golden Stairs' - were carved into the ice, allowing only single file movement up the mountainside. And it was here, on Palm Sunday, April 3, 1898, that tragedy struck the mountain. February and March had seen heavy snowfall at higher elevations, but the first two days of April brought warm winds followed by more snow. A few stampeders ignored the warnings of veteran mountain people and started up the stairs. During the night of the second, small avalanches began tumbling down the slopes burying 23 people. All of these were rescued, but the rumbling of more avalanches created a mass evacuation of the mountain slope. Over 200 people rushed down the mountain in heavy snow and near zero visibility – all kept together by a 200 foot rope. About a thousand feet below the Scales, the mountain side gave way and those at the front of the line were buried in up to 50 feet of snow. Approximately 63 people were lost to the avalanche.

Several thousand gold seekers headed to the Yukon over the 26 mile Chilkoot Trail. From the summit they descended a steep slope to Crater Lake then continued to Long Lake, Lake Lindeman and finally Lake Bennet at Carcross. Those who had climbed White Pass and those who had come over Chilkoot stopped at Lake Bennett to build boats for the journey to Dawson. Ice held on the lake until May 29, of that year and by the time it began to move over 7,000 boats were ready to go – destination - Dawson and the Klondike gold fields.

S.S. TUTSHI

The S.S. Tutshi was designed and built by the British Yukon Navigation Company as a tour boat for the Southern Lakes System in the Yukon. Launched in June 1917, it was 167 feet long with the original capacity to hold 110 but it became so popular that capacity was increased three times. In 1925, it was converted from wood burning to fuel burning. Although the main purpose was pleasure cruises, mail and freight were sometimes on the manifest. When tourism declined, Tutshi's career as a pleasure cruiser ended and in 1955 it was hauled ashore and abandoned. The Yukon government purchased it in 1972 and slowly began the process of restoration. While the restoration continued, the boat was opened in 1988 for limited tours. but was destroyed by fire in 1990. What is left of it has been salvaged and set up as a memorial display. The memorial cost $600,000 and commemorates the history of the ship and others that plied the waters of the lakes servicing communities and businesses that have been lost in the pages of time as she very nearly did.

Upper right – What remains of the SS Tutshi
Above -Charred timbers on the bow
Right – Howard Hess at the paddle wheel

WHITE PASS YUKON RAILWAY

Construction of the northernmost railroad in the western hemisphere – the White Pass Yukon Railroad – began in 1898 during the Klondike Gold Rush. It was the first major civil engineering project on the continent above the 60th degree of northern latitude and was the steepest pitch railway in Canada. From sea level at Skagway, it climbs almost 3,000 feet in 20 miles through terrain that some considered impossible to conquer. Built entirely by manual labor using only picks and shovels, crews used 450 tons of black powder to blast away mountainsides in order to lay rail on local lumber spaced on a 10 foot wide roadbed. Men were suspended by ropes to keep them from falling off while cutting the grade around 16° turns. The project included 2 tunnels, several trestles and bridges, one of which was a steel cantilever bridge 215 ft. high and 840 ft. long, which, when it was built in 1901, was the tallest of its kind in the world. Although that bridge was not completed until 1901, the rail reached the summit on Feb, 20, 1899 and Carcross in July 1901. Between then and 1982, White Pass operated trains as well as docks, ships, paddle wheelers, pipelines, hotels, airplanes, stagecoaches, sleighs, buses and trucks and pioneered inter-modal transfer of containers. During WWII, the railway was an essential transportation link moving troops and equipment to Alaska and Canada for construction of the Alaska Highway. When the mining industry collapsed in 1982, the railroad closed down. It reopened in 1988 for summer service only, taking tourists from Skagway up beautiful scenic White Pass to Fraser B.C. and Carcross, Yukon. In 1994, the WPYR was recognized as an International Historic Civil Engineering Landmark joining the Panama Canal, Eiffel Tower and Statue of Liberty.

The Duchess, built in 1878, was purchased in 1899 to provide transportation on the Taku Tramway. The two mile long tramway connected Carcross with Atlin B.C. There was no place to turn the train around so, on the return trip, it backed up to Carcross. The Duchess was retired in 1919 and moved to Carcross in the 1950's.

MONTANA MOUNTAIN

Montana Mountain is an ancient eroded stratovolcano created when an ancient tectonic plate - the Kula Plate, began slipping beneath the southwest Yukon. The mountain covers approximately 69.5 sq. miles and its highest peak – Montana – towers 6,286 feet above sea level – the 137th highest peak in the Yukon. The massive includes three other subpeaks: Brute - 6,117 ft., Matheson - 5,957 ft., and Dail - 5,545 ft.. Because it lies in the traditional territory of the Carcross/Tagish First Nation, they assumed ownership and stewardship of the mountain in a 2006 land claim settlement. According to the ancient legends of these people, Montana Mountain is one of the peaks that Game Mother used to hang a swing for her animal creations. Each animal sang and danced a different song while standing on the swing and afterwards Game Mother gave each animal their character attributes of today. With an abundance of plant and animal life, the mountain was also an important source of food, medicines and refuge.

The first gold and silver claims were laid out on the mountain in July 1898. Col. John Conrad created the biggest mining venture on the mountain employing 200 people. By 1906, the city of Conrad lay at the base of the mountain with hotels, stores, restaurants, bath and laundry houses, post office, churches and mining recorders office as well as regular steamboat service from Carcross. The longest aerial tram in the world rose 3,700 ft. up the mountain, extending four miles up to the mines to carry ore back down for shipment. In 1906 the tram cost $75,000 – 2016 cost would be nearly two million. By 1909 the town had all but been abandoned; the mines were shut down by 1914. There is no doubt that rich ore still exists in Montana Mountain but extracting it is made impossible by the geological make up of the mountain itself. Faults and fissures formed, closed and shifted with plate movement, resulting in intricate weaving of volcanic and sedimentary rocks through which mineral rich thermal waters filtered and settled.

CANYON CREEK BRIDGE

We called it the Aishihak River Bridge; built in 1904 when a road was built from Whitehorse to Kluane Lake following a gold strike the previous year that brought stampeders rushing into the region. It survived heavy traffic and raging spring floods until the 1920's when the government contracted for it to be rebuilt. In 1942, the 18th Battalion of the U. S. Army Corps of Engineers dismantled the old bridge and built a new one in 18 days – a replica of the old one. During 1986/87, reconstruction saved 10% of the superstructure and 85% of the cribbing. In 2005, the bridge was almost completely rebuilt and today it is in sad need of repairs.

HAINES JUNCTION

Coming into Haines Junction from Alaska on the Alaska Highway

Coming into Haines Junction from the south on the Haines Highway

Lowell Glacier in the St. Elias Mountains blocked the Alsek River several times in ages past creating a lake in the Dezadeash Valley that was, about 200 years ago, more than 60 miles long, covered over 97 square miles and was over 650 feet deep at the face of the glacier. Sometime around 1891, the glacier receded enough to release the waters of the last Lake Alsek. Scientists believe the lake emptied in 3 days at the same rate of flow as the Amazon River flows today. Haines Junction, established in 1942 as a construction camp and supply and service center during the construction of the Alaska Highway, is located on the bed of that recently drained lake. The Haines Highway between Haines Junction, Yukon and Haines, Alaska, was built in 1943. Between 1953 and 1955, an oil pipeline was built from Haines to Fairbanks with a pump station just north of Haines Junction.

Yukon Flowers

Northern Bedstraw

Photo courtesy of Howard Hess

Common Harebell

Arctic Lupine

Northern Goldenrod

Wandering Dawgs

Prairie Crocus

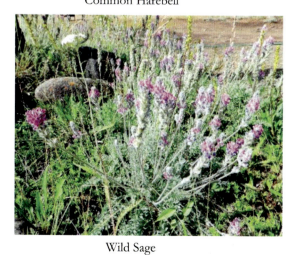

Wild Sage

Dog Violet

Daylight and temperature combine to create brilliant depths of colors and large sizes in far northern flowers. The optimum temperature for blooming plants is about 62° and the average temperatures in the arctic areas are in that range. At these temperatures, plants don't have to waste much energy cooling down – instead their energy is spent creating deep brilliant colors. Size of the plants and blossoms is created by exposure to 24 hour daylight.

Above – Fireweed blooms among the ruins of Silver City, Yukon

Below Fireweed turned to seed in the fall in Silver City.

A GLIMPSE OF YUKON WILDLIFE

Stone Sheep are a dark species of Dall Sheep found in southern Yukon and northern British Columbia. Rams weigh up to 250 lbs. and stand 40 inches tall at the shoulder. Color varies from dark charcoal to light gray brown with light faces and a white rump patch that extends down the back of the legs and belly to back of front legs.

Grouse – mating dance
Photo by Howard Hess

Photo by Howard Hess

Caribou

Alaska and western Canada were once home to the largest land animal native to North America – the wood bison. An adult bull weighs up to 2,250 lbs. compared to 1,900 lbs. of plains bison. By the middle of the 20th century, wood bison were thought to be extinct. In 1957, a plane crew reported a small herd of bison in remote northern Alberta. Investigation revealed that they were wood bison. Protected as an endangered species and aided by conservation efforts, the number of animals increased until over 11,000 now roam freely in Canadian forests. The Alaska Wildlife Conservation Center near Anchorage acquired a few and began a reintroduction program in Alaska, but the program faced two major hurdles. A small herd of plains bison was released near Delta during WWII and interbreeding would result in the loss of the wood bison. Since wood bison are listed as endangered, release would change the use of any land. To overcome this issue, the wood bison were listed as a "nonessential experimental" population. Finally, a small herd of 100 animals was released near Nome in 2015.

SHEEP MOUNTAIN

Sheep Mountain at 4,173 feet - the 123rd highest mountain in the Yukon - is located in the Kluane park system and towers above the Slims River at the head of Kluane Lake. It is home to about 200 Dall sheep with a life expectancy of 12-13 years. Long term studies have revealed that food supply is the primary factor in maintaining the herd at fairly consistent numbers. They compete for food with a large population of arctic ground squirrel and, on parts of the range, with a very small number of wild horses. Prior to the establishment of the National Park, human activities was the most important factor in sheep mortality rate. Coyotes are now the main predator; wolves are rarely seen. Other potential predators - bears, cougars, lynx, wolverine – do not appear to have an affect on the sheep population.

KLUANE LAKE

Established in 1972, Kluane National Park was recognized by UNESCO as a World Heritage Site in 1979 with focus on the glacier ice and snowfields of the St. Elias Mountains and some of the world's most spectacular glaciers. Lowell and Kaskawulsh Glaciers connect icefields which form the largest nonpolar icefield in the world and provide water to northern rivers and lakes. It is believed that the climate has changed very little in the Sheep Mountain area since the last ice age. Everything in Kluane Park is big: Canada's highest and most massive mountains – where the Kluane and Icefield Mountain Ranges make up the St. Elias Range. Canada's highest and North America's second highest peak - Mount Logan rises up to 19,545 feet. Kluane Park and the Kluane Wildlife Sanctuary in the Yukon Territory, the Tatshenshini/Alsek Park in British Columbia and the Wrangell/St. Elias National Park Reserve and Glacier Bay National Park & Reserve in Alaska form the largest single protected wilderness area in the world.

Kluane Lake, the largest lake in the Yukon, is approximately 37 miles northwest of Haines Junction. About 50 miles long, it covers roughly 100,000 acres at an average depth of 102 ft.; 299 ft. at deepest. Kaskawulsh Glacier meltwater forms the Slims River and the lake headwaters. The Kluane River drains the lake and flows to the Donjek, the White and then the Yukon to the Bering Sea. Kluane (pronounced "Klu – wah – nee") is a native word which means place of many fish and it does contain a good number of Whitefish, Burbot, Lake Trout, Inconnu, Arctic Grayling and Northern Pike. Inconnu is an oily fish found mostly in far northern waters. Little is known about the fish which can grow to nearly 5 feet in length and weigh up to 60 pounds.

Wind blown silt from upper end of lake

Only 8% of the park is forested because high alpine climates have extreme weather conditions which deter plant growth. Trees include: white spruce, birch, trembling aspen, balsam poplar, willows, alder, and, in higher elevations, dwarf birch. The largest diversity of flora north of the 60th parallel - around 220 types of arctic, pacific and maritime wildflowers - flourish in the park including: mountain heather, fireweed, arctic poppies, moss campion and purple saxifrage.

Park animals include North America's most genetically diverse grizzly population, black bears, moose, caribou, Dall Sheep, mountain goats, cougars, wolves, lynx, wolverines, muskrat, mink, marmot, red fox, otter, coyote, beaver, snowshoe hares and ground squirrels. More than 180 species of birds including bald eagles, golden eagles, mountain bluebirds, trumpeter swans, peregrine falcons, gyrfalcons, hawk owls, rock ptarmigan, magpies and Arctic terns have been seen here.

Destruction Bay

Sunrise over Destruction Bay

Along the shores of Kluane Lake lie two small communities – Destruction Bay and Burwash Landing. When I started driving the Alaska Highway in 1997, large yellow plywood dozers supported signs at either end of Destruction Bay - 'WELCOME TO DESTRUCTION BAY' on one side and 'PLEASE COME AGAIN' on the other. The town, I was told, started out as a construction camp and relay station for truck drivers building the Alcan Highway in 1942. Located at historic mile 1083, the site received its name when – according to the story - a young officer began building his camp along the lake shore against the advice of local native people. His newly constructed buildings and materials were scattered during a storm when high winds roared down out of the mountains above. Destruction Bay holds tenaciously to the location by the shore. There is one service station, one restaurant, one gift shop and one hotel – all in one. It is a rest, refuel and refresh spot on a lonely road. And it is still a highway maintenance camp for the Yukon road crews.

Highway Memorial

A family's loving tribute to a young life ended too soon – the loss of a son, a father, a brother , a friend. Wood and stone hand carved by a father.

BURWASH LANDING

Burwash Landing was originally a seasonal camp for the Southern Tutchone people who hunted, fished and gathered food in this area for thousands of years. A trading post was established in 1904 during the Kluane gold rush and a permanent settlement grew around it. When soldiers arrived in 1942, during construction of the Alaska Highway, they found an oasis in the wilderness complete with fresh garden produce and milk cows. The church and school was built in 1944 using abandoned Army structures. A new uniquely designed Catholic church was completed in 1974. Too large for the local congregation, the building was offered to the community to be used as a natural history museum. The museum, created by local residents, offers world class wildlife exhibits featuring realistic dioramas depicting over 70 native animals, birds and fish. A wildfire, in 1999, swept through the area threatening the whole community, but an all out effort stopped the fire just short of the old church. The community survived with the loss of only 5 family structures.

MT. CHURCHILL

The largest volcanic eruption in North America in the last 2,000 years came from the tallest land volcano in the U.S. - Mt. Churchill in the St. Elias Mountains near the Alaska/Yukon border. Ash from the eruption, which was 50 times the volume of Mt. St. Helen's 1980 eruption, was found as far away as Germany. Only one other eruption has covered the earth with ash that traveled 4,370 miles – Toba super volcano. In one massive eruption 75,000 years ago, Toba threw 670 cubic miles of ash out to smother South Asia, India and East Africa. Churchill's eruption, much larger than Krakatoa and Mount Pinatubo, ejected 12 cubic miles of ash. Although the volcano is in Alaska, the massive eruption left ash over more than 130,000 sq. miles of Alaska and northwest Canada. In the Yukon, those layers were up to 2 feet thick. The impact of the eruption, which included acid rain, pools of carbon dioxide and microscopic glass particles, was catastrophic to all life in the Yukon. DNA testing showed the spore of pre eruption caribou were genetically different from the post eruption caribou and as much as a 100 year gap separates the two.

Layers of ash are visible beneath the surface in road cuts along the Alaska Highway between Whitehorse and the Alaska/Yukon border, on the North Klondike Highway between Dawson City and Whitehorse and on the South Klondike Highway between Whitehorse and Skagway. It is also visible along stream beds and roadside lakes and ponds where melting permafrost is causing banks to break away and slip down as in the photo on the right. The stream in the photo below has left deposits of the ash on the bank after running at higher levels.

Although White River soil was first recognized by Lt. Fredrick Schwatka as volcanic ash in 1883, its source remained a mystery for over a hundred years.

In the 1960's, geologists traced the ash back to the St. Elias Mountains, but Klutlan Glacier blocked further exploration, leaving them to speculate which peak was the source. Thirty years later, a geological survey identified a caldera that was formed when the summit of Churchill collapsed during the eruption. Deposits along the rim of the caldera were chemically and mineralogically identical to the White River ash.

At a world conference in 2011, scientists from both sides of the Atlantic compared samples of ash from the Yukon, Nova, Scotia, Greenland, Northern Ireland and Germany and found them identical; all samples were from Mt. Churchill where the largest amount is found. For years, the European samples had been thought to originate from an Icelandic volcanic eruption.

ALASKA HIGHWAY

Photo by Howard Hess

In 1941, the government realized that Alaska was a pivotal land in the changing world but it was vulnerable. Military bases were quickly established in both Fairbanks and Anchorage and supply routes were laid for both land and air access. In March 1942, more than 10,000 soldiers with 250,000 tons of material began moving into position and a month later began the almost impossible task of building a road that would connect the lower 48 states to the northern territory. Seven different units, located in seven different areas, set to work moving both north and south. Six months later, in October, the last gap in the road project was bridged; in November, the 1,670 mile road was officially opened to military traffic. By the end of 1944, improvements had shortened the road to 1,568 miles. Further work has shaved the distance even more to 1,387 miles from mile 0 in Dawson Creek to Delta in Alaska.

Winter construction was difficult but keeping the road has proven just as much of a challenge. Portions of the road were built in areas where permafrost is close to the surface and, in the Canadian North, that is melting at an accelerated rate. The result is never ending wash board road surface, potholes, dips and frost heaves. Each year, maintenance of the 120 miles of road between Destruction Bay and the Alaska border costs nearly $22,000 a mile; a cost that is directly related to damage caused by melting permafrost.

Road construction, by itself, is one of the leading causes of permafrost degradation. A section of road just east of Beaver Creek has been set up to study several combined methods of thermal stabilization. The 12 subsections involve use of heat drains. snow/sun sheds, reflecting surfaces, air convection embankment, grass covered embankment and winter snow removal. Monitoring is done by means of 300 thermistors, 150 surface temperature loggers, groundwater sensors and weather monitors. Data is sent to a center in Whitehorse via satellite.

BEAVER CREEK

Canada's western most community - Beaver Creek - is a small town '301 miles from nowhere' according to a song from the days of the Beaver Creek Rendezvous show. It was here, on October 28, 1942, that two bulldozers – one working southward and one working northward – touched blades completing construction of the Alaska Highway. The town was founded in 1955 to service travelers on the road which opened to public use in 1947. The first time I was there was during construction of the trans Alaska pipeline back in the winter of 1974. I recall only a combined hotel/café/gas station where truckers swapped loads headed north to the oil fields. By the time I started driving tour buses in 1997, hotels had been built to handle the number of tourists passing through. Beaver Creek is the gateway to the Yukon and even boasts an international airstrip. Twenty miles west is the U.S./Canadian border and U.S. Customs.

The 647 mile border between Alaska and the Yukon extends from Mt. ST. Elias on the south to the Arctic Ocean and is maintained jointly by both the U.S. and Canada. While the 141st line of meridian was chosen as the border, marking it on foot up and down mountains, and across rivers, lakes and glaciers with a line in 1906, was a daunting challenge. In some places border markers are off by as much as 200 feet or more. It is marked only by an 80 foot cleared swath of land and boundary monuments shaped like the Washington Monument. There are eleven 5 ft. high monuments like the one near Beaver Creek, Yukon which is pictured above. The remaining 180 monuments are 30 inches high.

Yukon Winter

Liard Hot Springs in January

Klondike II in Whitehorse

Sign Forest in Watson Lake – cold and foggy

Ice Fall

Winter Sunset

Yukon Memories

Dawson Creek

Whirlpool Canyon

Howard in Toad River – "Water's not as cold as I thought it would be!!

Ariel & Joey at Ice Field Overlook

At Canyon City near Whitehorse on the Yukon River

Wading in Muncho Lake – and – yes – that's ice

2015 Trip with Granddaughter Ariel – Destruction Bay

Early morning Mountain reflections

Brilliant fall colors at Liard River Suspension Bridge

2015 Trip - Granddaughter Ariel and her husband Joey

Above - Million Dollar Falls

Climbing Rock Walls

Right – Liard Hot Springs

Tagish Lake

Cupcake Mountain – Haines Junction

Otter Falls – What a drive!!!

Yukon Tours

Top of the World Highway

Bear on tour posing for photo

Yukon tours often meant getting on the ferry at Skagway

Making sure we can get across flooded road

Somewhere on the Alaska Highway

At Miles Canyon near Whitehorse

Mud from Top of the World/Taylor Highways

Spring and fall might mean driving with little to no visibility

Bibliography

Carcross Tagish First Nation Parks and Recreation Branch Pamphlet
Canadian Journal of Earth & Sciences (1995)
Ancient Volcano Blows winds of Change - Yukon News (3-7-14)
The Milepost
Yukon News
ExploreNorth - An Explorer's Guide to the North
YukonInfo (on line)
Parks Canada
Travel Yukon (on line)
Yukon Communities (on line)
National Park Service – Chilkoot Pass

Karen Simon lives in Fairbanks, Alaska. She has driven tour buses throughout Alaska and the Yukon for 21 years sharing the beauty, the history and stories of the land she has called home since 1969. The awe of the Northern Lights and the stunning beauty of the land inspired her to paint, with winter Aurora scenes and whales being her favorite subjects. Mystic Alaska rose out of the desire to share all seasons with visitors by creating a single photo album; but it was their enthusiasm for the book that prompted publishing. And it is continued encouragement that spurred this project.

The author on tour in the Yukon

Some of the photos in this book may be available as photo, glass and canvas reprints. Information may be obtained by contacting chenamist@gmail.com

Other books by this author available on Amazon and Create Space include:

Mystic Alaska

I Believe – Old Churches of Alaska & the Yukon

Crystal Cove

The following books by this author were published by and available through Alaska Dreams Publishing:

Inside the Circle

Ghost Cave Mountain

Made in the USA
Middletown, DE
28 December 2022